Day Trading

─ ─ ─ ─ ─ ❧❦❧❦ ─ ─ ─ ─ ─

The Advanced Guide that will
Make You the EXPERT of Day Trading

Anthony Kreil

liable for any hardship or damages that may befall them after undertaking information described herein.

Additionally, the information in the following pages is intended only for informational purposes and should thus be thought of as universal. As befitting its nature, it is presented without assurance regarding its prolonged validity or interim quality. Trademarks that are mentioned are done without written consent and can in no way be considered an endorsement from the trademark holder.

DISCLAIMER

Although the author and publisher have made every effort to ensure that the information in this book was correct at press time, the author and publisher do not assume and hereby disclaim any liability to any party for any loss, damage, or disruption caused by errors or omissions, whether such errors or omissions result from negligence, accident, or any other cause.

Table of Contents

Introduction

Congratulations and thank you for downloading *Day Trading*.

The following chapters will discuss some of the most important things that you will need to know to be an expert day trader. This is meant for a person who is already educated about day trading.

You will learn about more advanced strategies and indicators to help improve your ability as a trader. The first things we will go into are technical indicators, if they are important, and how to use them for the best results.

Then we will look into contrarian and momentum trading. These are advanced trading strategies that will help a trader stay consistent in the money they make.

This book will also go into reading candlestick charts and other types of charts. These will help you to analyze the markets so that you make a better, more educated decision in picking your stocks as well as entry and exit points.

The last chapter will provide you with two stories of successful day traders. These stories will show you that it is possible to be a success in the trading industry as long as you follow the rules, and possibly have a bit of dumb luck.

Day Trading

There are plenty of books on this subject on the market, so thanks again for choosing this one! Every effort was made to ensure it is full of as much useful information as possible. Please enjoy!

Chapter 1:
Technical Indicators

Stochastics, Bollinger Bands, moving average, RSI, the MACD, and the list continues, but what are the best indicators when it comes to day trading? A day trader needs to act fast, so if you are trying to monitor too many indicators, it can take too much time. When it comes to day trading, things need to be kept simple. Follow only a couple of indicators max, or you could not follow any.

Consider the following to figure out the best day trading indicators for you.

To Indicate or Not to Indicate

Indicators are basically a manipulation of volume or price data. A lot of day traders won't use indicators. You don't have to use indicators to make a profit. You should practice trading based on price action and then you will find that there isn't much need to use indicators. That being said, indicators can help certain people notice things that aren't obvious.

An example would be if the price is trending higher, but it starts to lose momentum. To a person that isn't used to reading price action, this could be hard to notice, but indicators will give them the ability to see them. Unfortunately, there are problems that come with indicators which include showing a reversal at the wrong time. Indicators aren't good or bad one way or the other. They are only tools and therefore their usefulness depends on how you use them.

Redundant Indicators

A lot of indicators are pretty much the same thing with slight variations. One type could use percent movements and another uses dollar movement. Indicators could also be a part of the same "family." RSI, MACD, and stochastics are all examples of this.

While they may look different on the surface, typically only one is good enough. Using all of them won't give you any extra information for your trades because all of them are going to provide you with the same info.

Even a MACD and a moving average can provide you with the same info. If you were to use a MACD indicator as well as a 12-

and 26-period MA, they will both tell you the exact same thing. The only thing the MACD will show you is the distance the 12-period average is below or above the 26-period averages.

Once the MACD moves below or above the line of zero, the 12-period average has crossed below or above the 26-period. If both of these were on your chart, they would show the same thing.

If you are interested in using indicators, you should pick a single one from each of these groups. Even just having one indicator from each group could cause some redundancies and clutter and not provide you with any extra insight.

- Oscillators: The oscillating indicators will flow down and up, typically between the lower and upper bounds. The most popular oscillators are MACD, Commodity Channel Index, Stochastics, and RSI.

- Volume: These will normally mix together the volume along with price data to try to figure out the strength of the price trend. The best volume indicators are On Balance Volume, Money Flow, Chaikin Money Flow, and Volume.

- Overlays: These are the types of indicators that show overlap in price changes. This is unlike a MACD indicator where it separates from the price chart. You can pick more than one overlay since the functions vary. The most popular overlays include Fibonacci Extensions and Retracements, Pivot Points, Moving Averages, Parabolic SAR, Keltner Channels, and Bollinger Bands.

- Breadth Indicators: The last group of indicators includes those that deal with what the broader market looks like or trader sentiment. These typically only include stock-market-related information and include the Advance-Decline line, Trin, Ticks, Tiki.

You really don't need more than one indicator from each category. The only thing you could use more than one in would be overlays because they can help to indicate trend changes, trade levels, and possible support or resistance. If you master overlays and price action, you probably won't need any other indicators.

Combining Indicators

It's best to choose only a couple of indicators that will help you with your exits and entries. And RSI is able to be used to find the entry point and trends. During an uptrend, the RSI needs to extend over 70 on rallies and stay over 30 on pullbacks. This will help you to confirm trends, see when the trend direction may change, and highlight trading opportunities.

Moving average envelopes, ATR stops, or a moving average can be added to the chart to aid in finding exits. An example would be you could use one as a trailing stock loss on trades that are trending. If you notice a trend going up, try to figure out when to exit if the price were to fall under the line.

This is only a single example as to how indicators can be mixed together. The indicators that you choose will depend on how you trade and on your time frame. Make sure you calibrate your indicators to the specific strategy, timeframe, and asset that you are trading. An indicator comes with default settings, but they may not be in your best interest, so make sure you alter them to get the best signals for your trades that you take. Indicator settings could end up requiring adjustments on occasion as the market conditions start to change over time.

Unfortunately, there isn't a single indicator that will be perfect for day trading. These indicators are merely tools; they aren't going to give you profits. To make a profit, you have to use your price analysis abilities and your indicators the right way. This will take some practice. Whichever indicators you end up using, keep yourself to no more than three—even zero is okay. If you use more than three indicators, it becomes redundant and could end up costing you money.

Make sure you know everything about your indicators. Are there any drawbacks? When does the indicator normally produce incorrect signals? What are the good trades that it misses? Does it often give signals at the right time? Will the indicator trigger a trade or will it just tell you about a possible trade? It's important to know these things about your indicators, and you will be well on your way to making a more productive use of them.

Chapter 2:
Contrarian Traders

As you could probably guess from the name, the contrarian trader will trade against the big market trends. They will always look to purchase assets when they aren't performing well. They will then turn around and sell them when the performance starts to get better.

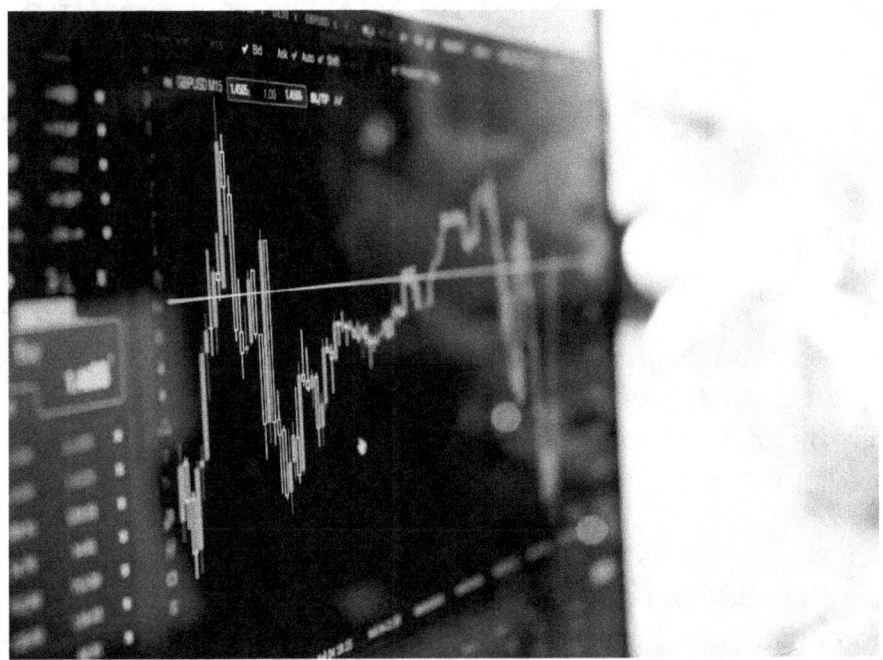

Contrarian traders normally believe that the ones that say the market is going up tend to only do that when they are completely invested. This means that they don't have any more purchasing power. Similarly, a person who thinks that market is at a downturn normally have already sold out, suggesting that the only way the market can go is up.

These types of traders will use a lot of investor sentiment indicators, especially the ones that emphasize out-of-favor securities like ones with low P/E ratios.

A contrarian investor doesn't always go against the larger investor pool or public. If a stock is trending higher, it doesn't mean that the contrarian trader will automatically stay away from the stock. Instead, these types of traders will try to find the stocks that the public sentiment runs against the established trend. The best stock for the contrarian trader would be stock that is going up in price, even though there is an increasing amount of pessimism among the majority of the other traders.

Indicators

Contrarian traders will keep an eye on the market and the market news to make sure they assess the broader sentiment. A trader that chooses to follow a contrarian strategy should rely on analyst ratings in order to gauge where other investors are landing when it comes to a certain stock.

If a stock's price is going up but there aren't very many "buy" recommendations, a contrarian trader will likely see a lot of potential. Contrarian traders will also use options and shorts so that they can profit from the declines in price. Contrarians will also normally use volatility index, put-call ratios, sentiment surveys, and more. They will also assess their own reactions when it comes to analyzing data.

There are a lot of contrarian traders that want to make a profit from overvaluation situations that they have looked at, foreseen years or months in advance of all the other markets. This tends to be lucrative because the majority of markets will typically fall a lot faster than they go up. Nevertheless, there are a lot of active traders that have a lot less time to assess, make, and hold trades that they think may be profitable. Using technical analysis can be extremely helpful when it comes to optimizing their entry and exit from short-term positions.

The technical contrarian trader will normally try to find the market tops, and will generally use a specific price action clue or indicator that tells them that a market extreme may happen, and then they can combine that with analysis that shows them the deterioration of waning demand or upside momentum.

Benefits and Risks

The contrarian trader has a pretty good chance of being very successful, provided that they keep in mind that action and opinion are extremely different. They should also remember that trends tend to be where the money actually is and that you need price confirmation to know that there is a reversal.

When it comes to being a contrarian trader, there are five dangers that you have to watch out for.

1. The momentum that is going against you could be more powerful than you think.

    Contrarian logic is that once the prices get too high, they have to come down, and prices are too low, they have to go up. But there is also logic in momentum trading. After investors begin to lean in a certain direction, they will more than likely follow the herd.

2. **Contrarian investing can be lonely.**

This type of trading looks amazing on paper, but it's harder to pull off. Humans are influenced by those around them. Contrarian traders tend to only hold a position for a limited time, but to gain success, you have to be free from normal human thought. Don't expect to have too many other people who will view trading like you do if you follow a contrarian strategy.

3. **The crowd can sometimes be right.**

Sometimes the crowd isn't right, but there are times when they are. Stocks prices will normally continue to fall far below fair value when there is a possible huge bull market. Even though contrarians think things should be turning around now, they probably aren't right.

4. **Big gains will come at the expense of the other traders.**

The contrarian trader will get the best gains when there are lots and lots of other traders that are making huge mistakes. They are serving a purpose by doing this. The act of contrarian investing helps to balance out the markets. Contrarians can't help but get excited when they start to see the prices go up extremely high or extremely low. These extremes are when the contrarian trader does the best work.

5. You could end up outsmarting yourself.

The contrarian trader has to be smart. But they can end up being too smart. You've probably heard the saying "It's not nice to fool Mother Nature." Well, there is the similar quote when it comes to trading: "It's not polite to believe that you know where the market is heading before it goes." If you start to think that you have everything figured out, you will find yourself being tempted to profit from the reality that what rises will fall. You will also be tempted to profit from your genius ability of "knowing when" this price change is going to start falling.

The very best and most famous contrarian traders have laid down a lot of money on their successful buts, but it tends not to be that simple. The successful contrarian has to make sure that they are well-researched, and they have to be extremely confident in what they are planning on doing.

Chapter 3:
Momentum Trading

A momentum trader will look towards the acceleration in the price of stock, or they will look at the company's revenues and earnings. The trader will then decide to take on a short or long position in the stock hoping that the momentum will continue to follow that direction. Because of this, the momentum trader is very similar to the trend trader, although they do tend to rely mainly on short-term movements instead of on the fundamental particulars of companies. Momentum trading has a history of being known as hard to be successful. This means that it is a branch of trading that only the experienced trader will try their hand at.

When a trader is making a momentum trader, they will time their sells and buys based on how quick the stock is currently moving. Unlike the majority of other traders and analysts who like to focus on the fundamentals of a company or technical analysis, the momentum trader is mainly interested in the things that are going on in the news. They want to find the stocks that are moving by a high volume or percentage.

To be a successful momentum trader, you have to have a high level of attention and focus. They have to say steadfast when they catch some momentum in the right direction but the target hasn't been reached. Because of this, these types of traders have to have a large amount of discipline.

There are a lot of day traders who choose to be momentum traders, and you typically won't find other types of traders or investors that follow the momentum plan. Timing is the most crucial thing to be a successful momentum trader. When you look at the broad category of momentum trading, you will find at least two small subgroups: event-based momentum traders and technical-based momentum traders.

Technical-Based

The technical-based momentum traders will make their decisions based on their perception of whether or not the market is higher or lower than they expect. They make use of technical analysis to figure out their assessments. If this type of trader was to see that the market price is higher than they think it should be, they will short now and then buy later. If they find that the price is lower than what they thought, they will buy now and short later.

Event-Based

The fundamental-based momentum trader will base their decisions on the volatility of the market which comes from the news and other activities that are going on throughout the trading day. When the market is smacked with a big piece of news, the market will normally react with the volatility increasing. The volatility increase will normally continue for a few hours. Momentum traders may try to make their money through several quick trades in the places where there is fluctuation.

Strategy and Techniques

The momentum trader focuses on more than stock trends. They look to find stocks that have a strong move in a certain direction, typically ones with high volume and over a certain period of time. They will then buy the stocks that have been trending in the direction they just found, in the hopes of capturing waves of investing enthusiasm which have temporarily prompted new lows or highs in the market.

Traders that use the momentum strategy will typically draw their analysis and data from these types of techniques and sources:

- Daily watch lists

  The momentum trader will normally follow daily watch lists of their stocks, and they will normally stay glued to brokerage apps, message boards, televisions, and more.

- Volume as indicator

  A trader that chooses to trade based on momentum will follow the trade volume as their biggest indicator. If a stock has more buyers than sellers and it starts to gain popularity, the price will normally go up, and trading activity will continue to increase.

- Resistance levels

  After they have found a stock that is trending in a particular direction, the momentum trader will try to find companies with stocks that have resistance levels that are being tested. If the stock were to break the resistance level in either direction, it becomes a prime candidate for a person to trade.

- Technical indicators

  For a trader to find a resistance break, the momentum trader will look for technical indicators. There are some trading programs that analyze trend lines automatically. Momentum traders aren't as concerned about selling at tops and buying at bottoms. They will instead make their moves based upon a price trend after a stock has completely and clearly passed the resistance point. They will then sell or short the stock once they have reached a profit.

- Conservatism as a grounding strategy

  A momentum trader must fully understand when they have to cut their losses. They are always looking to gain some small profits every day, but there are sometimes times when their momentum trades don't work. When this happens, it would make sense for them to get out of a position than to continue to hold onto it hoping that it will possibly turn around. Still, a good trader that is adept at working through resistance points is able to trade with a decent amount of safety. Still, there is always some risk that comes along with trading.

- Trading times

  Typically a momentum trader will focus on the first and last hour of the trading day. During this time there is a lot of action which will give them higher volatility. They will also make sure that all of their positions are closed at the end of the day. If they leave a position open overnight it can end up causing unexpected changes to their momentum.

- Discipline

  Discipline is crucial for the momentum trader. They will normally follow one or two stocks, and they have to have quick reflexes to react to the market. They will often have to use margin so that they generate a decent amount of profits, and this will increase the risk that they take.

Determine Momentum

One of the best ways for a trader to figure out the market momentum is by using the Average Directional Index indicator. A reading that shows a figure below 25 tends to indicate the market will provide strong pullbacks to start a swing trade. If the reading shows a figure of about 25, it tends to indicate a trend with a minimal pullback. The best momentum trader will look for an ADX level of 25 or more.

The main reason why momentum trading is successful is that the best-performing stocks will normally continue to outperform the majority of the market. The main reason for this is quite known, but it could be because of irrational behavior by investors and her mentality. It could also be because of the fact that some of the companies have better management than the competition. In truth, momentum traders really couldn't care less about the reasoning. They are only looking to have the best way to analyze the market for finding and trading stocks that they think have good momentum.

Dangers of Momentum

There are some risks that come along with a momentum trading strategy. If executed properly, it has been linked, in some cases, to a trading type known as high-probability trading. Still, if the momentum trader was to get into a position too early and it ends up turning out that it doesn't achieve its momentum, it can present a problem. Similarly, if a trader were to close a position too late after it has reached a saturation point, this will minimize the trader's profits. Also, if the momentum trader were to end up missing a news story, they could end up missing out on a big investment opportunity.

A momentum trading strategy is considered to be a more difficult approach to trading, but the possibilities for its significant profit is extremely high. This is especially true because momentum will typically be the single greatest factor in the movement of the price of a stock.

Momentum traders will make use of a short-term strategy that helps them to profit off of a stock's high-volume movement. These types of traders will try to find breakout points in price and then they will follow them with their trade. They will normally close out of all of their positions before the end of the trading, and they will make use of margin to help support their gains. This really is a trading strategy that is very spur-of-the-moment, which will require a lot of analysis and super quick reflexes, so this trading strategy is typically reserved for the more advanced trader.

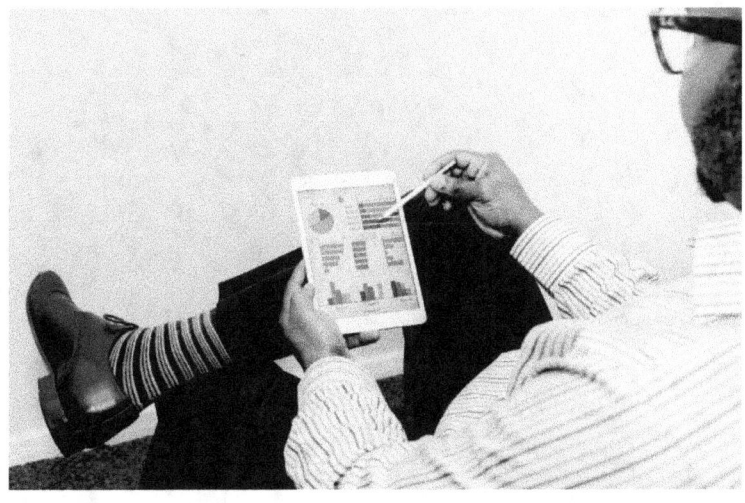

Chapter 4:
Reading Candlestick Charts

Munehisa Homma, an 18th-century Japanese rice trader, is credited for the creation of the candlestick chart. It's believed that his methods of using candlestick charts were further adjusted and modified throughout the years to become more useful for the current financial market. Steven Nison brought the candlesticks to the Western world through the book *Japanese Candlestick Charting Techniques*.

Candlesticks have now become a staple for every trader's trading platform and charting programs for every single financial trading vehicle. The amount of information and the simple nature of the components makes these charts popular among all traders. The ability to connect several candlesticks together to find the underlying pattern makes it perfect tool when you need to interpret forecasts and price action history.

How to Read

When you look at the candlestick, you will see that it is broken into three parts: the body, the upper shadow, and the lower shadow. The body will be red or green. Every candlestick represents a certain time period. The data found in the candlestick summarizes the trades that were executed during that certain time. An example would be if you were looking at a five-minute candle, it represents five minutes of trading data.

A candlestick holds four data points: the close, the low, the high, and the open. The open tells you the first trade of the time period you chose, and the close will tell you the last trade of the period you chose. The close and open is what makes up the candle's body. The high tells you the highest price the stock traded at in that period, and the low is the lowest price that the stock traded at in the period.

The high on a candlestick is represented by a vertical line that extends from the body's top to the highest price, which is called a shadow, wick, or tall. The low is then represented by the lower tail or shadow, which is a vertical line that extends down. If the stock closed closer to the open, then the body will be green telling you that they made a net price gain. If they open higher than the close, the body will be red, showing that the net price declined.

Patterns

Each candlestick shows the fight between the bears and the bulls, sellers and buyers, greed and fear, demand and supply. It's important that you remember that the majority of candle patterns have to have a confirmation based upon all of the earlier candles and the candle following. Beginners will often make the mistake of seeing one candle formation without looking at the whole context.

For example, hammer candles show you that a near-term capitulation bottom if the candle forms once there has been three preceding bearish candles. If a hammer candle were to form on "flat" sideways candles, it is pretty much useless information.

This means that it is helpful to understand the complete story of every candle so that you can get a complete picture of the mechanics of the chart patterns. These patterns normally continue to repeat themselves, but the market does try to fake out the traders in the same way when you overlook context. A candlestick chart is most often representational of emotion due to the body's color. It's extremely important that you make sure you use a mix of other indicators along with your candlestick charts so that you get the best results. The following candlesticks are some of the more common reversal patterns.

- Hammer Candlestick

  A hammer candlestick is a bullish reversal. This is probably the most-followed candlestick pattern. This reversal is used to figure out the capitulation bottoms that come after a price bounce that traders use to choose when to enter long positions.

  A hammer will always form at the end of a downtrend and tells you when a stock is at a near-term price bottom. This candle will have a lower shadow that will make another low in the sequence of the downtrend, and then it will close back up near or higher than the open. The tail, or lower shadow, has to be at least two times the size of the candle's body. This will show that the longs finally gave up the last of their positions and stopped out as shorts began to cover their position and the bargain hunter will start to come into play.

Seeing a volume increase helps to solidify these types of hammer. In order to confirm the hammer candle, it's extremely important that the following candle closes above the low of the hammer candle, and preferably above the body. The best signal to buy would be seeing an entry that is above the high of the candle that followed the hammer with trail stops beneath the hammer low or the body low. It's important that time your entry with a momentum indicators such as RSO, MACD, or stochastic.

- Shooting Star

A shooting start candlestick is a bearish reversal, which tells you a peak or top. This candlestick is the exact opposite of the hammer candle. The start needs to appear after at least three green candles, which indicates a rise in price and demand. Eventually, the buyer will end up losing their patience and will chase the price to a brand new high before they start to realize that they have overpaid.

The upper shadow or wick needs to be, in general, twice the size of the body. This shows you the last bit of frenzied buyers that have entered into a stock just when profit takers have unloaded their position, which is then followed by short-sellers that push the price of the stock down to close the candle close to or below the open.

In essence, this will trap the late buyers who allowed themselves to chase the price too far upwards. Fear is struck at the highest point since the next candle needs to close at or below the start candle. This will cause a panicked selling spree as the late buyers will panic to get out of the losses. The typical signal for a short-sell will form when the low of the next candlestick price has been broken with trail stops the body or tail high of the shooting star candlestick.

- Doji

This is a reversal candlestick that can be bearish or bullish depending the candlesticks that came before it. The candle will have the same—or at least close to it—open and close price with long shadows. It will look a lot like a cross, but it may also have a small body. The doji candlestick represents indecision. The doji is typically a reversal candle, and because of this the directions of the candle before it is able to give early indications of the direction that the reversal will end up going.

If the candles before the doji are bullish, then the following candle will end up closing under the body low, which will trigger a sell/short-sell signal as the doji's candlestick low breaks with a trail stop higher than the doji high.

If the candles that came before the doji are bearish, the candlestick will more than likely form a bullish reversal. The long trigger will form higher than the body, or the candlestick high, and will have a trail stop under the doji's low.

- Bullish Engulfing

The candlestick is easily seen by the large green-bodied candle that completely takes over the full range of the red candle that came before. The bigger its body, the more extreme of a reversal it becomes. The body needs to completely engulf the red candle that came before.

The best bullish engulfing candlesticks will show up at the end of a downtrend so that they trigger a quick reversal bounce that will overwhelm all of the short-sells, which will cause a panic short covering buying frenzy. This will end up motivating the bargain hunters to come in, and this will further add to the buying pressure. These candles are potential reversal signals of downtrends, and they also show a continuation of uptrends when they end up forming after a shallow pullback. The volume needs to spike to at least double the average when these candles form to make sure they are the most effective. The buy trigger will form once the following candlestick goes beyond the high of the bullish engulfing.

- Bearish Engulfing

Much like a huge tidal wave completely engulfing an island, a bearish engulfing candlestick will swallow the green candlestick before it. This will indicate a strong price reversal. The body of the bearish engulfing will eclipse the body of the green candle that came before it. The strongest bearish engulfing candlestick's body will consume the total candlestick includes its shadows. These types of candlesticks can be signs of huge selling activity that was brought on by a panic reversal from bullish to bearish.

The green candle that comes before it will keep the unassuming buyers optimistic. These candlesticks will normally open up higher, which will give longs hope for a bigger climb as it starts to indicate a more bullish market. However, the sellers will come in extremely strong which will drive down the price through the opening. This will end up causing some concerns with the longs.

The selling will continue to intensify as the price begins to fall through the low of the previous close. This will then trigger more panic selling as most of the buyers from the day before are now underwater. The selling continues to grow into the candle close because most of the buyers of the previous close now have a loss. This reversal is extremely dramatic.

This type of candle is a reversal candle. It creates an uptrend as it causes more sellers the following day as the trend begins to reverse into a breakdown. You will see a short-sell trigger when the following candle exceeds the low of the bullish engulfing. On downtrends that exist, this candlestick may end up forming from a reversion bounce, which will resume the downtrend at a faster speed because the new buyers were trapped at the bounce.

Just like will all other candlestick patterns, it's extremely important that you observe the volume, especially when it comes to engulfing candles. The volume needs to be at two times more than the average trading volume of the day to have the highest impact. Algorithm programs tend to paint the tape at the close of the day with some misticks to close the day out with a fake engulfing candle in order to trade the bears.

- Bullish Harami

The bullish harami candle works in the opposite direction of the bearish engulfing candlestick pattern. The large body of the engulfing candle comes before the small harami. The engulfing red candle that comes before the harami needs to be a capitulation candlestick where the low point of the sequence shows a capitulation sell-off before the harami, which should be position well within the range the large candle.

The subtle small body helps to keep the short sellers in an unassuming mode because they think the stock will fall again, but instead, it will stabilize before it forms a reversal bounce that will surprise the short seller as the price reverses back up.

The harami candle is very subtle and will keep the sellers unassuming until the trend will slowly begin to reverse. This candle isn't as dramatic or intimidating as the bullish engulfing. The subtleness of this candle is why it tends to be dangerous for the short seller as the reversal begins to start slowly, and then it will accelerate quickly. The buy long trigger will form when the following candle comes up through the high of engulfing candle before it and will stop once it is placed under the harami candle's low.

- Bearish Harami

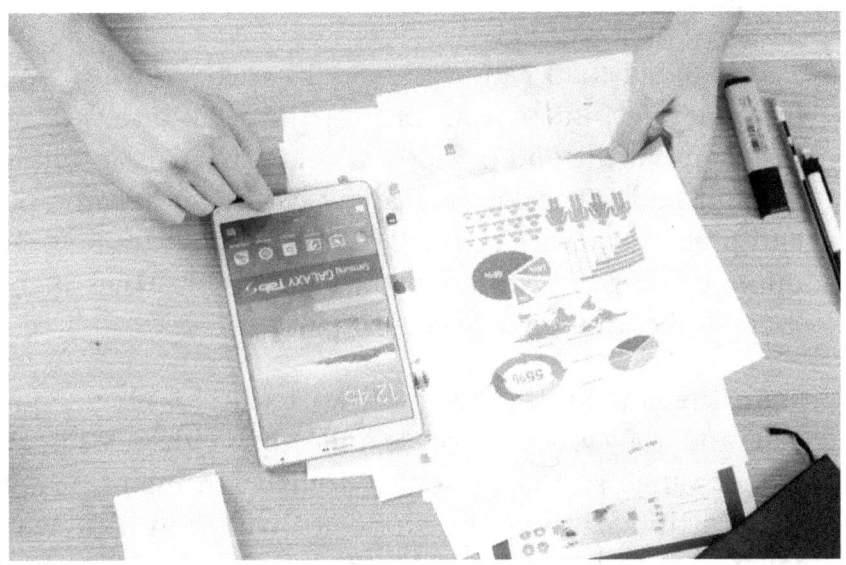

A bearish harami candlestick is the inverse of the bullish harami candlestick. The engulfing candle that comes before the harami should complete eclipse it. The will always for at the beginning of an uptrend as the green candle that came before makes a brand new high a big body before the harami candle is created as the pressure to buy starts to go away. Because of the slow nature of the buying slow down, the people in long positions will assume that the pullback is only a pause before the trend starts again.

When the bearish harami closes, the next candle will close lower, which will then begin to cause concern with the logs. Once the low of the engulfing candle is broken, it will cause panic sell-off as the longs rush to get out of their positions to prevent any more losses. The normal short-sell triggers will start once the low of the large candle is broken and the stops can be added higher than the high of the harami.

- Hanging Man

The hanging man candlestick looks pretty much identical to a hammer, but it will form at the peak of an uptrend, instead of at the end of a downtrend. This candle will have a small body. The lower shadow is larger than the body, and preferably twice as big. It will have an extremely small upper shadow. It's different than the doji because its body is created at the top of a range.

With the candle, the buyers thwarted a possible shooting star and they brought the candle up to the close at the higher range so that it kept a bullish sentiment, which is often artificial. However, the truth will then hit once the following candle closes under the hanging man because the selling will accelerate.

Hanging mans will normally be more effective at the peak of the curve of the price spike that is composed of four or more green candles. The majority of bearish reversals will form on doji and shooting starts. Hanging man is a very uncommon candlestick because they are a sign of a big buyer that ends up getting trapped when they try to support the momentum, or they try to pain the tape in order to cause more liquidity.

Hanging man candles normally signal a possible peak of an uptrend as buyers who ended up chasing a stock end up wondering why they chased it so high. The short-sell trigger is signaled when the low point of the hanging man is broken with the trail stops added higher than the hanging man high.

- Dark Cloud Cover

This comes after a three-candlestick reversal, and the dark cloud cover will create a new high for an uptrend sequence because it will gap above the previous candle's close, but will end up closing in the red as the seller will step in early.

This will show that the longs ended up anxious to take protective measures, and they sell their positions even while the new high is being made. The dark cloud cover needs to have a body that closes lower than the mid-point of the previous candles' body. This is how you can distinguish it from a doji, hanging man, or a shooting star.

The previous candle, dark cloud candle, and the next confirmation candle will make up the three-candle pattern you need to see. The candles that precede need to be at least three consecutive green candles that lead up to the dark cloud cover.

The selling that happens will overwhelm and trap the brand new buyers. If the following candle does not make a new high, something above the dark cloud cover, then it will create a trigger for short-sells once the low of the third candle is broken. This will give you a trap door that will indicate a panic sell as the longs will try to get out of the failing traders to prevent further losses. The trigger for short-sell is signaled when the low of the third candle is broken, with the trail stops higher than the high of the dark cloud cover.

Chapter 5:
Charts

W hen it comes to trading charts, there are four main types of charts that are commonly used by traders and investors so that they can understand the movement in the markets.

- Intraday charts

- Weekly charts

- Monthly charts

- Daily charts

These different charts will show several different ways that the price movement is shown over a certain time period. This can be used to look at price movement over several different time periods. You will begin to see that your view of a certain market has the ability to change in a drastic way only by changing the different time horizon.

Monthly Charts

These trading charts will show you the price movement over the long-term horizon. Long-term investors are the ones that most commonly use monthly charts, and they will most often show several years or possibly even decades of the price data for their chose market or security.

Traders don't typically use the monthly charts because the time horizon that it shows doesn't always provide them the most popularly traded times. This, however, doesn't mean that a trader can't find use in them. In fact, there are a lot of market "gems," or a representation of a certain era, that are always added to a monthly chart. It's important to remember that these types of charts are more commonly used to look at time periods that go beyond four years.

Weekly Charts

Much like the monthly charts, the weekly charts are often used by investors and traders that have a long-term time horizon. These weekly charts typically come in handy when a trader needs to analyze the intermediate-term time horizon. It's important to remember that weekly charts are more commonly used to look at periods of times that exceed six months.

Daily Charts

The daily chart will show the price action of one trading day of activity in a market. Daily charts tend to be most commonly used by investors and traders. These are extremely helpful when it comes to analyzing the intermediate to short-term time periods. There are a lot of traders that will use the daily charts to help them with long-term analysis too. It's important to remember that the daily charts are more commonly used to look at the periods that exceed six weeks.

Intraday Charts

Intraday charts are extremely popular for the trading community, along with the daily charts. The intraday charts show what the price movement of a certain market is within the parameters of the days open and close of the market.

While there are loads of different ways to look at intraday charts, the following are the more commonly used intraday charts.

- Intraday Hourly Charts

  These charts will show the hourly breakdown of the day's trades. Each hour will show the open, close, low, and high of each interval.

- Intraday 15-Minute Chart

  These charts will show a 15-minute breakdown of the day's trades. Each interval will show the open, close, low, and high of each 15-minute interval.

- Intraday 5-Minute Charts

  This is the most common chart that is used by day traders. Each of the intervals on the chart will show the open, close, low, and high of every five-minute interval for the given time period. These charts are most commonly used for people interested in quick scalps, or for day trades that go on for several minutes to several hours. The five-minute chart has become popular for the longer-term trader when they are looking to efficiently pick their entry and exit points.

- Intraday 2 Minute Charts

This is another common chart that day traders use. Just like the others, each interval will show the open, close, low, and high of a two-minute interval. These charts are popular for scalping, or for trades that go on for several minutes to a few hours.

- Intraday Tick/Trade Charts

Tick charts, also called trade charts, are line charts that will show every trade that the market executed. Time isn't involved on the tick chart. Every point on the line represents a trade that happened on the market. In markets that aren't liquid, the lack of trades will be shown by a flat line. In markets that are very liquid, the tick chart will constantly move, and will track every trade with a line across the time, and will go up or down to show the increases and the decreases in the stock's price. These are most commonly used by scalpers, but people will use them to track "out of the money" trades that need to be fixed.

The way a trader views the market will change a lot depending on the time period that they choose to look at. To get ready for the trade, the analysis of the right time frame is imperative. For example, if you are looking to scalp the market, it doesn't make sense for you to look at the monthly chart. Neither would it be smart to look at a five minute or tick chart for a long-term core position. Technical analysts, traders, and investors will tailor their expectation out of the market to work for their certain time frame.

Chapter 6:
Time Management

For a trader who decides to trade part-time, it can be rough. While everybody would love to think about electronic markets trading all the time beginning at a big advantage, they have to admit that it comes with its hindrances. Just because there is a market open doesn't mean that the time a trader chooses to be present is the best time for them to trade.

Nor does it mean that a person will have the time to completely analyze the market the way that it needs to be and make the best decisions based on what they were able to learn. The window of time that a part-time trader has is pretty small, and there are very few people who can adapt to trading philosophy around this while they also find a way to make things work.

Managing their time tends to be the biggest roadblock for most traders because they aren't quite used to a fixed routine, not to mention the learning curve, experimentation, and trial and error that gets in the way of clean consistency.

Connected closely to risk is time, and it is an issue that has to be catered to each trader's personality type. This means that if your personality type likes the quick thrills and is typically made up of very little patience, the trying to trade part-time is going to be a lot harder to accomplish.

Locating short-term opportunities each day can be simple when the bulk of your day is spent on analysis. Even still, those high-probability trades that are based upon the trader's strategy tend to be scare during the trading session. This means that attempting to pack a full session where you typically find yourself flat in an hour or three hours with distractions will be that much harder to focus on what it is that you need.

The bad trader will typically be full of holes, but those holes tend to be nothing more than a lack of knowledge, both long-term and current. Without enough time, finding the right information can easily be missed, which will put the trader at a big disadvantage. The following five tips will help you to work in the right direction when it comes to making sure that your time in managed right.

1. Sync up your trading philosophy so that it matches your personality and the time you are available.

   There are so many traders that will try to trade with a program that works completely against every fiber of their being. There are lots of factors that could interfere with their thinking, and time tends to be one of them.

   Are you the patient type? Do you have problems staying still and being antsy? If you are an antsier person and you are a trader, then the best option that you have is to adopt a short-term strategy that you are able to deal with comfortably in the time you have devoted to trading, and then you will have to force yourself not to overdo things. This means that you need to take on short-term trades, but make sure that you don't overdo things in terms of the number of pairs you trade. A good analysis will take some time, and if you tend to be all over the map when it comes to the information that you can absorb during a single session, you are more than likely overdoing things.

If you tend to be patient and systematic, then you are pretty well suited for longer-term goals. You may choose to use limit orders for execution, or could easily drift into longer-term fundamental or technical plays. Take profits and stops are big and the risk is normally a lot lower. People that don't have enough time may prefer a strategy that is longer-term because they simply don't want to be there to watch every single tick. The full-time trader that chooses to use long-term strategies is typically invested across several different currencies, which adds more diversification.

Whether you have a personality that works for short-, medium-, or long-term trading strategies will depend on you. Regardless, this needs to be your step on with your step two focusing on making sure your strategy fits into the boundaries of time that you have.

2. Don't sacrifice sound analysis.

The one area of trading that you want to make sure that you don't skimp on is sound analysis. Traders that choose to omit important information are doing nothing more than blindly staring at charts and making an ill-informed guess as to what could happen next.

Take the bit of time that you do have and make sure that you fully absorb the analysis. If you aren't able to make the time to completely study the context of your pairs, then you should not plan on trading these pairs. It is crucial that you have sound analysis. Make sure that you use your time wisely, and that you only execute once you have a very high level of confidence.

3. Dig deep and make sure that you avoid distractions.

Phone ringing like crazy, TV blaring, looking at the general news sites, or looking at YouTube are horrible things to have when trading. Just like with all other types of work, these things pose a huge distraction risk, and they are the fastest way to deter people from being able to obtain the important information that you will need in order to make the best execution. Make sure that you use the time that you have and get rid of all the distractions that can pose a threat to clean, deep, and concise analysis that is required in order to make progress. Shut your office door, block out all of the noise, and stay focused.

4. Adopt a systematic way to take in the information.

Traders that tend to be unorganized when they make their analysis or just click through from one topic to another, will end up confused and scattered. It's best if you start with a reputable new site. These are news sites that provide you with the big picture on what's currently happening. These should be on the top of your bookmarks list.

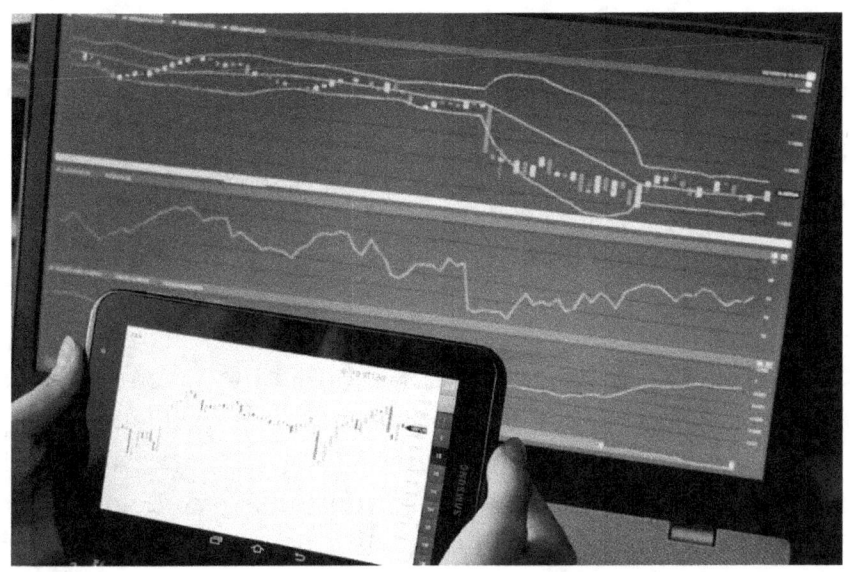

When it comes to looking for specifics, you will want to drill into your intraday news feed. Start looking at correlations and other markets so that you can come up with a well-rounded knowledge bank for your situation. After you have made a general determination that you are satisfied with, then you can begin to dive into charts. Look at several timeframes and then break things down into small pieces.

While you don't have to follow a strict top-down analysis structure, it helps to begin with the macro picture and then try to break things down into small parts. There are deficiencies in the traditional top-down analysis. If you make decisions based solely on the macro view, and that view ends up wrong then everything that comes after is a wash and you may end up setting yourself up for something bad to happen. You should keep a global approach and know that the market timing is just as important as all the other areas.

5. Don't try to force a window of time.

The biggest rule for risk management is: Don't do anything at all. Simple? Pretty much. Commonly followed? Not really.

If you like to have a short window time when it comes to your average trade length, you need to make sure that you understand what could come along with it. There will be days when you aren't comfortable with any trades, regardless of the amount of time you have to spend analyzing things. Analysts work as publishers and always try to force activity down their reader's throats whenever they can. The bottom line: if you're not able to make money from the things that you understand, then you should not make a trade. You need to enjoy trading and all that goes with it, so don't try to force a trade when you know things are right.

Chapter 7:
Success Stories

The Corporate Trader

Steve spent 25 years working for a large company. He liked the job, but eventually, it started to wear him down, and he got burned out. He was talking to his dad one day and told him that if he could do anything for the rest of his life it would be to trade full time. His dad told him to go for it, and he did.

Steve had been doing investing and trading work as a hobby for a few years. He had also started to day-trade on Fridays, which were his days off. This is how he discovered he enjoyed it. The great thing was that if he needed to, he could go back to his old job.

After almost being tricked into losing a lot of his money through a trading education company, he found Active Trader. He took a course through the website and signed up for the active trader chat room. He began to break even with his trade, but still wasn't making money. One day, somebody asked him if he had read *The Playbook*. He hadn't, and he didn't know what SMB Capital was. This is what turned his day trading career around.

When he started following the SMB blog, he had a "Doh" moment when Mike talked about finding your strengths. He took an SMB class and it changed his life.

After he finished his class through SMB, he only had seven losing weeks, and never experienced a losing month. He typically makes a profit four out of five days each week. Every profit he has had he increases his trade size by 10%.

But Steve's story comes with a warning from him. Don't think this was easy. It wasn't. He put in an average of 65 to 70 hours each week between taking classes and trading. And he continued to work for 55 to 60 hours each week after his class ended. He says it's also important that you remember that you can always get better.

The High Schooler

Back in 2014, Conner decided to play sick and stay home from school. He holed himself up in his room and opened his laptop. During the summer, his dad had given him an E*Trade account with $10,000 that Conner had earned over the last two years.

He had originally put the money into well-known companies like Apple and Verizon, but this day he chose to liquidate those positions and put almost all of his capital into American Community Development Group. This was a penny stock that sold for $0.003 a share.

Throughout the next year, his $10,000 grew to more than $300,000, mainly through trading penny stocks. While a junior in high school, he would use his iPhone to buy and sell his stocks during lunch, in the bathroom, and sometimes during class.

Conner has always been interested in making money. When he was a kindergartener, he dressed up as a concession boy for Halloween. He even had a tray which had candy and popcorn on it. His mother said that he came home with money and no candy. Then he started selling lemonade. They live in a cul-de-sac, so very few cars ever came near their home, but Conner didn't care.

At 14, he got a job as a busboy and worked on the weekends. All the money he made into a savings account, but he wasn't happy with the interest that it earned. His grandfather convinced him to give the stock market a try, and his father, a former Wall Street trader, agreed to be the custodian for an E*Trade account.

Conner was a fantasy football fanatic and had a head for numbers. He tried out online poker and sports betting, and he got into trouble with his parents when they found out. Penny stocks gave him another outlet for that risky reward-seeing behavior.

He picked ACYD because he had heard that the CEO was planning to announce that he would buy back shares of the company in order to get the price up to a cent per share. Conner bought several positions, and then four days later the company made the announcement of the buyback program, and the price shot up.

At the close of September, the shares hit a little over a penny in price. This made Conner's portfolio worth $50,000. Then the price hit six cents and his portfolio reached just under $200,000. At the end of December, Conner sold most of his positions, and by that time the stock was gone back down to four cents per share.

Conner had applied to college and planned on studying entrepreneurship, economics, and finance. He is also a fan of Tim Sykes, who runs a chat room for day traders that specialize in penny stocks.

Conner was also running his own website to help others get started in the day trading world. His parents made sure that his website didn't end up sounding like he is promising people the ability to get rich quick. He shared his process and the stock he's looking at but doesn't make big promises.

Conclusion

Thanks for making it through to the end of *Day Trading*, let's hope it was informative and able to provide you with all of the tools you need to achieve your goals whatever they may be.

The next step is to use the information you have learned in this book and apply it to your day trading strategy. With more information, you can make better choices and ensure that your gains stay consistent.

Finally, if you found this book useful in any way, a review on Amazon is always appreciated!

www.ingramcontent.com/pod-product-compliance
Lightning Source LLC
Chambersburg PA
CBHW071240220526
45468CB00002B/941